VESPERS ON POINT REYES

Selected Poems
1989-2019

Peter Weltner

VESPERS ON POINT REYES

Editor: Clarinda Harriss
Graphic Design: Ace Kieffer
Author Photo: Nathan Wirth
Cover Photos: Nathan Wirth

BrickHouse Books, Inc. 2019
306 Suffolk Road
Baltimore, MD 21218

Distributor: Itasca Books, Inc.

ISBN: 978-1-938144-62-2

Printed in the United States of America

For Gerald Coble

Table of Contents

I

McAdoo Farm

Life begins surprisingly sometimes, the way
paradise appears out of nowhere, out of nothing
but the ordinary, the world as it is on a day

when the sun is also young, its golden morning
hiding behind trees, hickory and pine,
while a boy drives down Westridge, listening to Elvis sing,

past ranch houses and a few last farms, the shine
of dawn brightening as he enters the battleground
waving at the statue of General Greene on his equine

mount, its unpolished patina mossy and browned
as the field where for centuries soldiers have lain.
He turns right at the drive-in theater, goes southbound

on a wooded road, reaches the McNairy domain,
a big white clapboard house, a gentleman's dairy
with a black angus herd where he manages to restrain

from blowing his horn since Walton must be sleepy
from last night's football game. His heart is racing
as the boy pictures him lying in bed. He passes slowly,

stares at his window, speeds up where the fencing
ends and the lake begins, heads for Church Street,
and reaches Gerald's at McAdoo farm. It's spring

everywhere. All is blossoming, May incomplete,
more bounty to come. Ezra, Gerald's stray,
named for Pound because found the day the poet

was released from Saint Elizabeths, wanders away
from his offered hand, sniffs weeds, turns around,
looks toward the woods, not interested in play,

untamed, half feral, free. He watches him bound
over the fallow field toward a long row of cane
and the forest beyond and turns down the sound

on his car radio though he listens until the refrain
is done, without a love of my own–no one,
poor guy–then clicks it off, his teenager's pain

that he must not tell anyone about like a stone
in his gut. He knocks on Gerald's door. More music.
What piece is it? If he knew, he'd feel less alone.

A George Arnold hangs over the couch, Antarctic
inspired, two bands, sky, land, the upper blue,
the lower reds and oranges, no impasto, never thick

but translucently brushed. In the studio, the work is new,
Gerald's recent paintings on his floor and walls,
strict horizons, pointillist foliage, a few

in casein evoking pebbles in brooks or waterfalls
splashing on granite or searchlights on a runway.
All landscapes. Vocation, his dad claims, is what God calls

you to do with your life. But he has nothing to say
of his own, can only imitate, pretend to be
who he is by mimicking, like a radio deejay

mouthing the words to a '45. He can see
only what he has been taught to see, a chameleon,
what is worse, a chameleon cliché, unfree,

whose colors match whatever branches it stands on
as it waits for the morning sun to warm its blood,
lizard-uncertain if it will survive to the next dawn.

Only others' eyes can show him what is good,
like Gerald's as he patiently watches him paint
in a different style each Saturday. It is understood

he'll play records, not talk. The boy's musical saint
is Berlioz, but today Gerald chooses Shapero's
Symphony for Classical Orchestra, not a faint

Stravinsky rip-off or Schoenberg minus the tone rows
but Haydnesque in its wit and melancholy.
The boy is liking it more each time it re-plays. It shows

in his work, Gerald says, grabbing his shoulder. "See?"
And possibly he does, in the peculiar blue in his sky,
with too much earthbound green in it to be

the less real one outside. He doesn't intend to lie.
Maybe he does look deeper.   But further below
he has nothing to see, just dark, too scared to reply

to the warmth of Gerald's hand. He doesn't know
what to say, how he should feel. Gerald removes
his grip, sits on his checker board table. He must go.

It is late, mid-afternoon. He is paint-spattered, shoes,
jeans, shirt. He has his father's lawn to mow,
a date that night. He leaves slowly as a tree's shadow moves.

It is too soon for him to love. Not cold, or callow,
just fearful of the truth, of what no one approves
of in his world when on that day sixty years ago
a boy knew what a man's touch meant and all his life to follow.

Randall Jarrell

He: "Pussycat." And Mary: "Pussycat."
Across the Burke Davis' picnic table,
purring, mewing, emitting little bat

squeaks, other creaturely endearments, able
mimics, too, of robins, sparrows, jays
metamorphically changed to animals in a fable

he might have written for one of his days
at the library, telling children tales
of adventures in their own backyards, the ways

owls and ducks, spades and watering pails
have of becoming us, we them, as he tugs
on his long salt and pepper beard that never fails

to provoke some child to shout, "Santa!" Even the bugs
in his stories are adorable sometimes. At a party
he gives for his step-daughter, his den's rugs

pulled back for dancing, he makes all of us be
still for a while as he plays the second movement
of the Mahler Seventh on his record player. And we

do listen, hard, trying to be as intent
as he to every sound, his wren-like eyes
surveying the room, eager for our assent

to the music's night noises. In our ears, it dies
away to the buzz of tree frogs, locusts, crickets
outside. A neighbor's dog barks, then howls. He sighs,

grimaces. There is pain in the air, the sound of threats
from who knows where, further than the nearby yard,
a cry that rises from the ground no one forgets,

no one who has heard its voice. Like the fabled snow leopard
in one of his poems, it appears, then departs.
As childhood comes and goes, leaving us scarred

for life, he says, shrugging. Tearfully, he starts
up the stairs, turns around, grins, waves good-bye.
I'm ten when my black cocker Duke darts

across the hilly street where we live and I
watch as the delivery truck strikes him dead.
For days and days I do nothing but cry.

I hear him yelp at the first blow still. My pastor said,
to comfort me, that God's creatures never die,
that all will be well. And Randall on the road where he fled

to in Chapel Hill, waiting for cars to speed by
like a deer on a highway, checking behind, ahead
before crossing until headlights blind it. Why
does it leap by instinct led into that bright eye?

Reunion

I can't go back. The youth I loved too much
is more lost than I am. Polluted by pet feces,
the lake is long closed to swimming. Trees
are chopped down, farm land now lots, the names
on mailboxes never the same ones I knew.
Not even the woods remain wild. New paths
have replaced those I took, though the light
the leaves filter at noon looks almost as golden.

Like his hair. I see it shining everywhere,
still long to touch it as I did that day after
school and an October rain, the sun pouring
through the porch screen as he and I, just
fourteen, watched on TV the face of a boy
young as us shot on a street in Budapest.

A Last Letter to John Baird

Manhattan frigid, you, I, and Barbara, bar-hopping,
Elaine's, some dive across
the street, tinsel decor, moss
fringing the windows, drinking without stopping

until it was midnight and I said good-bye, the next
day my interview at MLA
for a job, the city a gray
blur in my eyes as, tight, I worked to recall the text

of the letters I'd sent to schools, struggling to
sober up, to clear my head
by reciting the books I'd read
for my thesis to myself while thinking of you,

as I did all during the play we attended together
three days later, Hadrian
VII with Alec McCowen,
your knee pressing against mine, the weather

outside like an Antarctic storm, white-out, ball-
shrinking cold, you said,
as you left me, half led-
on by the copy of Sheeper you'd loaned me, the total

praise you'd lavished on Jack Smith, smitten
by you, thinking, despite
Barbara, the others, you might
be gay, inviting you down, after you'd written

me you'd nowhere to go, to Crescent Beach
my last lazy summer before
I left for that unknown shore,
for San Francisco where I'd gotten a position to teach

at State, in our motel, the third night, you standing
at the foot of my bed, knowing
I must be awake, showing
me what I wanted to see, that's all, landing

on your feet, so to speak, after our wild pub crawl
in Myrtle, early in the morning
finding a girl, I nothing
to you in the way I wanted to be, the sexual

wall between us unbroken, unsaid, your body
still so like a teen age
boy's and yet with rage
in it too, some will to hurt yourself or me,

the girl you'd been screwing out of your hair you declared
as I drove you to the airport
where, like a good sport,
you kissed me on the cheek and I waited and stared,

as if you hadn't been with me at all, till your plane
took off and I started my car
and drove for five days, as far
as I'd ever drive, hitting the city at the insane

end of the hippie days, and we still were writing, talking
on the phone, you with nowhere
to go as always, no care
for tomorrow, reading Burroughs, Genet, walking

the wild side, as Reed sings, of Manhattan, pretty
as little Joe, then one night
you asked to live with me, tight
friends as we were, and I said yes too freely

and when it came time, you needing the money
for the ticket I said no,
said fast I had to go
since I was in love with another guy and you and me

I never did understand, the flirting the books
the sly innuendos amidst
the girls the women, and I'd kissed
you once with no response, no dismissive looks,

no words, just your turning away and so I hung
up and heard later
from friends you were happier
alone but I knew even then it was wrong

of me, that I had betrayed you, that it was despair
that made you call me
and afraid of the responsibility
I'd refused, and suddenly you were taking care

of an old gay alcoholic in upstate New York,
Bobo, long retired
from our college, hired
way back in the 'teens, who liked to pop the cork

off champagne bottles too often and fondle his boys,
you maybe the last one,
generous, a bit of a stone
head, but kind, bright, annoyed by the noise

around you of fools, reading your half-mad writers
yet keeping your cool, always
contending how it pays
better to play at life than to be one of its fighters,

my hearing, two years after, rumors you'd died, young,
just over thirty or so,
I never did know
how or why, like a precocious poet unsung

in his grave, you, John, too late now I ask you
for forgiveness, who denied
you, who meanly lied
to you when I said yes and meant no those too

many years ago and I crazily in love
with you yet, still wanting
you who are haunting
me as I lie in bed in the motel room I think of

most when I think of us, you standing at its foot
again like a messenger,
not thinking of the girl, of her
but of me, and I and you equally mute,

nothing to say, and you, though an angel borne out of the sea,
won't free me or take me away
but silently declare I must stay,
here, in the exactitude of my desire, in my failure's clarity.

First Love: August 1959

1.
Behind the library, the names that are chiseled
into the granite gravestones are the pale gray
of faded tattoos. Sunlight scrambles easily

up ancient trees that are bent, grizzled
with moss, gray caterpillar tents, rai-
ded by borers. The air is too hot to breathe, yet breezy.

2.
Jays hide behind shadows like bats in the back
of caves. His day is a promise he has made
to break it, a lazy meal, a long wait for mail,

a stranger berating him at the store. He finds a sack
of kittens thrown into the Yadkin. Should he wade
in to save them? Crud crusts a squirming tabby's tail.

3.
A can of chicken soup, egg whipped in,
poured over bread. A Dr. Pepper.
A hunk of cheese. Honeysuckle

sticks to the house. A yellow, thin-
ly painted, soaks the blistering plaster
where two beams and a rafter look bound to buckle.

4.
An orange tastes sweeter than honey on
his tongue. Summer is thick with salt
on his skin, the bitter sweet sweat

of his body assaulted by the heat, the sun
in August. The dry thunder is at fault
for bringing no relief, no rain yet.

5.

The morning air is rippling. Sun-white
soil, the sky a blue glaze. Sharp, tall
grass, frazzled leaves. Cooling

shade, shadows, shutters. The fight
to find relief, the light hitting him like a wall,
like the strong waves of a storm at last incoming.

6.

Drifting past, new clouds are white as smoke,
dead cinders, furnace ashes. The sky's
gunmetal gray. The purged air gleams

like light off copper. Twigs from oak,
sycamore, pine litter the water ris-
ing in gutters, the rain-heavy streams.

7.

The earth's steaming, as after a fire's
put out. Porch swings creak. Moths cling
to screens. Tires splatter the road's shoulder.

He moves his bed nearer the window. Choirs
of tree frogs, mosquitoes that sting,
howling dogs, the smell of trapped mice left to molder.

8.

Bat cry, owl cry. The buzz of insects
against the windows. Leaves rustling
in the spare night breeze. A pickup, four

on the floor, parked off the road. They have sex
deep in the woods. Locust rasping.
His black hair. His jeans spread-eagled on the forest floor.

9.
Jesse and him at his home shooting the breeze
after, playing cards, listening to '45s,
smoking, talking about plans after school,

bragging about the future, distant seas,
foreign cities, what their lives
would feel like if guys quit being cutting and cruel.

10.
He sees two suns when he shuts his eyes.
As one descends, the second rises.
He lies alone on his drooping mattress.

He is happy. The cloudless night's sky's
on fire with stars. August hypnotizes.
Jesse and him. Him and Jess.

Herkimer Dolomite

1.
Hunched, arthritic, his clothes reeking from
cigar smoke, an old man visits the Sig house
bearing tweeds, an itinerant tailor who sews
suits, jackets, slacks for young gentlemen,
his fabrics woven only from highland wool,
he says, their colors a subtle heather, thistle,
loch blue. No buyers. He shrugs. Times change.
He stacks his goods in the back of his coupe,
drives down College Hill Road, his cloth bolts
lined up like rolled up banners behind his seat.
Twilight late in January, the sky's bronze as if
rusted by age, a lustrous deep coppery brown,
like decaying leaves or the campus's gothic
buildings, their stones smoldering in near dark.

2.
Its deep pits are quarried out. What rock's left
to mine is ironless, won't rust, stays dull gray
through years of weathering, not worth cutting
into blocks to fix what's chipped or cracked
on the college's ancient edifices, stained by
two centuries of northern New York ice storms.
I first saw them in spring, boys playing lacrosse
in the quad by the chapel, the morning light
casting the dorms with a ruddy patina, sun
soaked, like the mid-May tan on the guys
pitching, catching the ball with their racquets.
Odd how vividly I recall them that one time,
three months before I enrolled, like a picture
revisited in a year book, as clear to me now

as October's glory days, the Mohawk Valley's
dense woods turning to bloody maroon,
scarlet, flare red, fiery gold, flickering
yellows like a shrine's votive candles, hearth

flames slowly dying to November embers,
ash pale or flake white. Winter began soon
as a day or two after each Thanksgiving,
a few trees left clinging to no more than
a swatch of leaves, losing them by the first
snow, the sky watery gray like smoke from
a dampened fire. In upstate, winters are hard,
long like those in Arctic zones. But the old
hewn blocks thrive in cold. Their colors
deepen, blushed by the rust burning in stone.

3.
Michelangelo carved to free bodies lost,
hidden, forgotten in marble. He knew
stone memories endure way past our own.
Too many to name them all, profs, friends,
but I'll risk a few: Crossett, Teddy, Lady
Ed, both Cams, Kit, and you I loved most,
though we seldom talked the days we could–
the boys, men dead as always before,
their spirits chill as College Hill winters.
No matter the season, the buildings glitter
like crystalline snow. But their sparkling façades
hide rock's deep veins. Say life also rusts
like iron to a color bronze as late Brahms.
A quarried music. Our mineral companion.

Battenkill

It's famous. "Best trout fishing stream in America."
Here, the river doglegs, forming a pool Eakins'
boys would have loved if they'd lived near, flat,
man-sized rocks to sun on, a hemp rope, high
as a silo, tied for years to an old oak branch
still able to support two or three grown men
swinging over the waters, frothy where deepest,
to dive or cannon-ball in. Summer is such
a kingdom on the Battenkill. Idling bird song.
Folks on inner tubes floating by. Beyond Gerald's
and Bob's, it curves past bridge and silent mill.
In the corner of yards, on the border of farms,
headstones stand erect or lie half-buried,
well-kept or moss-covered, some chiseled with dates

older than the Battle of Saratoga. Small American
flags, some wind-shredded, memorialize the fallen.
Its planks peeling like infested redwood, fathomless
pits gaping between boards, a barn forms
a backdrop of sorts to a terrace, one of three
edged by brush and rocks, that descend to the water.
Fenced on both sides by fragments of stele or bits
of monuments no longer standing or long torn
down, its path narrows like an isosceles triangle
to a point where a girl's beautiful head carved,
etched from granite rests on a tall wood plinth.
The woman who posed for it now is dead, lying
only a few miles away under her own stone,
guarded fancifully by giant sculpted dogs.

Memory is a heraclitean flow none can cross
the same, unchanged, each time. I barely met
her, spent much of our one afternoon together
talking Faulkner with her and her husband, saying
how in his art landscape, place, is always part
of us and the past races past us faster than

the future can try to catch up–or something
like that. Who knows anymore? The face she wore
was an old woman's graced by joy like Hals'
Malle Babbe, an owl, wise to age, also darkly
perching on her shoulder, the girl she was
and is in the sculpted portrait still visible, as if
life were endless, streaming like the Battenkill
under winter's ice, fighting to stay river.

Michael's Gift

A plaster cow and donkey, five sheep, one chipped,
two shepherds chopped from pine, their crooks
twisted oak limbs, the magi garbed in silk ripped
from old scarves. Joseph's badly faded. Mary looks
downcast with re-painted doll-like eyes. The baby
Jesus is wrapped in cotton swaddles. The palms
are plastic. So is the manger in the cave. Michael can see
it is backlit like a stage, not by the star. What qualms
he feels as he ponders the shoddy nativity scene
in the church yard are not calmed when his mother
whispers in his ear, "It's Christmas, son. Hell's
been shut down for heaven-bound folks like us." Mean-
ing what? Could it be really true there is another
world less sad than this one? Be good, he's told, or else.

He is bullied at school, called a gay boy, a faggot by
the tougher guys. He never wants or means to stare.
They beat him with willow switches, make him cry,
leave him hurt and dirty in an arroyo. He doesn't care
his teachers think him lazy during classes.
He is tall, strong, but hates to fight and knows more
than other kids, stumbles sometimes, wears glasses,
boasts he doesn't believe in God anymore, would implore
Him to make them quit it if he did. Is it selfish
of him to pray for himself when he doesn't even try
to stop abusing himself? Maybe he'll die. It's absurd
the world is unkind. "Make a wish, make a wish,"
his mother says. "It's your birthday." With a sigh,
he blows out the candles. They must know, have heard

of why he is bullied. It's past time. He runs away,
leaves Corpus Christi to the morons, takes a bus
to Frisco, crashes in a pad, is invited to stay
in a derelict Victorian where gay hippies fuss
over him like a baby. He needs to escape
after a few days. What they do is sin. He'd lose

his soul if he were to succumb. "God's what you make
of yourself," his mother had said. "What you choose."
But he has chosen to defy her the Christmas I meet
him in the Capri, nursing a ginger ale. Great genes,
I think. In my bedroom, naked, only a cross
round his neck, he begs me to let us greet
the new year together since the crowd scenes
in gay bars scare him. All that noise. All that loss.

We date for three months. It's fine. I don't know why
I feel it won't last long. He finds a job in Fields Book-
store, likes to cook, go to movies, hike, try-
ing the back trails in west Marin. He is very good look-
ing, though he isn't persuaded when I say
so. But I tell him to leave anyway. I stop calling
him, quit dropping by his room on a bay-
side alley off the Embarcadero. Everything
I do is hurtful. I'm just one more mean school
yard bully, a cold, blaspheming, uncaring lover
who abuses his love by looking for another
better than him. Better than Mike? From the letter
he writes after he has gone, I know I'm a fool.
He has enclosed the cross he wore, no less a believer.

May each of us, at the end of our days, be spared
the wrath of our cruelties, the rage of memory's
curse, reminding us of our unkindness, those who cared
for us whom we failed. We, who do only what pleases
us, may we be forgiven for not loving enough,
for achieving only what was convenient,
what desire sought, who believed we could bluff
our way past death and need never repent.
In our last hour, relieve our minds and souls
of our hard words, each unkind, uncaring thing
we have said and done, you, who are music, who sing
in imagination, the angel old fables say controls
our final moments, save us as we die, preserve
the love, the gifts we were given and didn't deserve.

White Water Wind, #10

Sixteen, I jackknife off a board, hit my skull
on a rock in mud. The last thing I see is the sun,
the lake I am drowning in translucent as air.
Water man shadow dream. Wiping a mirror clean
of steam after a shower, dripping, erect, Bob
drops his towel. A full moon rains onto the bed
in our underwater room where he swims with me
past pleasure. Just over our heads crests break.
White water wind. The surface ripples in lunar
light, pale as a fire's last ashes, the cinders
too hot to touch. Desire is a torch that blazes
brightest when submerged, however dark the sea.
Dive to him. Water is freedom. Water is peace.
In the deep, gold gleams. Best of all things is water.

A Song of the Earth

I found today in the park clasped round the trunk
of a giant fern tree a metal bracelet embossed
with the name of an old Chinese lady I had seen
many times walking backwards down a path
for exercise, clapping her hands. You can hear,
if you like, in bark creaking in the wind, the crack
of falling limbs or cones, the cries of birds
startled by gusts from a Pacific winter storm
or rain pouring on an ancient fern's fronds
the music of her leaving a world she loved.

Can two hear the same in their listening? You,
me in our darkened rooms, straining our ears
to the "Ewigs" of Mahler's Das Lied as partiers
nearby carouse in Coit Tower's parking lot.

Last Things

Backing into the long line of tourists waiting
for a place to park in Coit Tower's lot,
a truck hauls off the last pile of rubble:
shingles, crushed boards, a flattened cum-stained
mattress, a zebra shade, linoleum tiles.
The bulldozer's blade has missed only a wall
grate, your Bekin's t-shirt, a work boot.
Soot black rats escape into a fennel patch
near the fig tree where jackhammers chisel
into pebbles the remainder of the retaining wall
that fell during the storm when, his house
slipping down a Tiburon hill, Kai-Yu Hsu
asleep in his bed was smothered by sludge
that poured through his windows like plaster.

Laguna Beach

His knotted strawberry blond hair is covered with sand,
his bathing suit cut-off jeans. His lesions are raw,
livid on both thighs, one zigzagging his left hand.
He is coral pink from sunburn, red as a crab's claw.

He knifes his name in rock face, cutting deep,
not satisfied until he knows it can be read,
then dives in, swims out past where the shelf is steep-
est, beyond the surfers, invisible except for his head.

Wait for evening to shade the beach, the first stars
to show, though you really must let him go.
He'll not return. It is like in the time of the wars.
People vanish, are listed as missing. But you know.

Wander like a spirit up and down the coast.
Perhaps you might meet again. Perhaps it is wrong
to write as he did after he learned he was lost:
This is the last story I'll ever tell you. So long.

My Mother in Her Dotage and the Kindness of the Lord

She hefts her dress up, tugs on her right stocking,
exposing a thigh and her diapers. The Beauty Queen
natters on about her victory in the 'thirties, shocking
no one anymore. Sid Cone insists he's just seen

the ghost of his cousin Claribel, but he seems
to have mistaken her for Gertrude Stein.
The widow in black tells each detail of her dreams
as if she had spent the whole night shopping. A fine,

strapping old man is prompted to sing a hymn.
He swings his arms as if he means us all
to join in. Some do, from table to table, at the whim
of the moment, until everyone, the whole dining hall,

is singing "Abide with Me" and my mother is crying
not at the song but at her loss of dignity,
her hair unbrushed for days, her hearing aids buzzing,
urine dribbling down despite her diapers. "To be

old," she whispers to me, "is horrible." And I think
of her and my father, making love, making me.
It was in their pleasure my life began. Sink,
I'd say to her, sink back, drown now in that ecstasy.

Woodlands, a True Story

Woodlands miles from home, backcountry,
a blue, shiny lake, a cabin abandoned
in the war
from which I still pilfer images
as if mine to keep. Photographs, calendars, muddy
shoes, yellowed letters, an earthenware
jar. It's the flailing heat of summer's end
when I hike through hickory,
oak, over grassy ridges
toward a clearing. Far off thunder, scary
to a kid. Damp humus.
Slippery red clay.
Thickets of vines to rip
past, brush to push
my way through, kudzu and honeysuckle.

That is how my life began, the first day
of it. Moccasins slithering
through water, skaters zigzagging,
gnats darting, rush-
ing aimlessly about as gusts grow fiercer,
birds circling
the lake while they struggle
to fly in strong winds, diving,
blessing the water as angels might do with a dip
of their wings, the sharp, peppery
odor of resinous pine.

All this, this world is little
more than air and dust now,
like the aftermath of a storm's big blow
that felled the oldest trees
by the edge of the meadow.

Yet in every sip
or breath I take it's in me.

The taste, the smell
of it, the rustle of leaves, the snap of twigs
as he steps toward the bank,
hunkers, drinks,
his uniform filthy,
rank,
his too long hair the color
of khaki, and limps off,
restored to the forest,
the wounded soldier
I've spied on, handsomely tall,
drinking while locust whirr
nearby, crickets chirp
beside him, birds swirling overhead
in a backcountry
a boy was too young, too small
to hike so deep into, yet stirred
into longing by
its trees, brush, high grass,
late August's darkly clouding sky.

And now I, still,
am bound to woodlands,
to its pine, oak, beech stands,
belonging to that place,
the groves, the hills,
the limestone caves I hid in,
each a part of me
as memory
is a desire to see
on my body
wounds, a face
mirrored by a lake I stare into,
its water lit
afterward
by twilight
as evening winds make new waves
bending the reeds,

the weeds I stand in yet
since all I write, that's mine,
repeats no more than this: this glimpse
I had of him
on the first day of my life.

Poem Set to a Line and End Words by Wordsworth

Touch–for there is a spirit in the woods.
Surprisingly, as if unexpected, the end came.
I'd climbed Mount Tam. Now it is old age
that shocks, the vast view witnessed for an hour
or two from the summit, then, the holiday
over, the trek back down, the Marin woods gone
more like a lifetime, the reason I came
across the Bay to Phoenix Lake overpowered
by a desire to be lost in a forest I never forgot.
A little boy, no more than four or five, I'd been
allowed to roam in woods freely. Maybe they said,
Why fear getting lost if you live as trees live?
I don't know. I became a city man and thought
an occasional trek up Tam was enough, to intrude
far back where trees, uprooted, crash and die.
Now, I'd return to the ancient stands, not from hope,
not according to necessity, Anaximander's thought,
but to smell the acrid pine resin bleeding, to be
young again, fearlessly lost in woods, not his,
the boy's, not anyone's, the sun seeping through a green
dark as moss or lichen, the rot and humus depth
enough for him as he rested and searched above
the canopy, beyond the sun, to find the spot
where his breath, the light came from, the source of desire
in trees, in him, his old man's small boy's godward gaze.

Redwood

Bald trees, no limbs to climb, foliage gleaming in a shaded light,
as snow shadows day, while you try to see far away
though only what's near is clear, vision intensified by
exactitude, this leaf, that needle, bark scrap, naked trunk:
whatever's more precise than memory in the back of an eye.

Think of Barnett Newman's zips or Pollock's Blue Poles,
how you dance to the rhythm of what they envision.
Consciousness must betray itself to be free,
must trust the ghosts concealed in things outside it,
these redwoods half seen, though no less certain, in shades of
gray.

How quiet the wilderness is today, wet from dew, the mist
that perpetually falls in woods, the murmur of a distant rain
that is part of what you know, is you, the light muted
by the moisture dribbling off redwoods, brush, and vines,
the music of a rainy morning's hushed musings, its silence
broken.

Or perhaps this is noon, this burnished gray, blackened
brightness,
not the sun's, but a gift of the primeval world you enter
with your camera: illusionless, stark, half-awake dreaming trees
as depicted on an ancient paper scroll, washed in watery ink,
nature
painterly, the cold, fading light you'll sleep better by deep back
in the forest.

A Walk Down Mount Tamalpais

Show me a stand of pine to find peace in, Lord,
a shape to the world more than my eye imposes
or my ears transpose from birds, wind to voices
no one can hear but me. My life is wandering.
Chance may place rocks in the wilds to reveal
a grace no choice can compose. A hiker lost
in dark woods might be afraid, but morning
will unveil which path to choose. My way is closed.
Thirteen when I lost my faith, I set myself on
a mortal quest. Old age would come and I'd
be done, having learned what I'd sought, all God
had wrought on this earth, and I'd be willing to go.
Is it too late? In ancient Colonus, death brought
one blind to an olive grove. I wait by the sea.

Stone Altars

The black rocks are for where the images fail,
for where the living lie buried
with the drowned among uncarved
stones. Flags are unfurled on ships once they sail

far from harbor or appear over the horizon,
piratical like those
you saw as boys
when they came for you, dark as these rocks. The sun,

luminescent, fills the sky with promise of return, the ground
of the sea bright as a mountain's
slope, the west sunset-lit like plains.
Beyond them, everything is silence, no sound

left in the world. Two gnarled rocks, a beachside cairn,
two fragments of one boulder fallen
into the sea, a common phenomenon,
though these mark old lovers who took care

of poor strangers, of whose devotion to the wayfarer
no more remains than two stones,
like relic holders enclosing bones,
that rise like the jagged back of a deep-sea creature.

Unsatisfied by the villagers in the valley below
the cliffside cottage, hungry, disguised as beggars,
two gods knock on their door. The couple, slow
to answer because of their age, the fear that mars
all late in years, invite them in despite
the rags they wear. The odor of their filthy skin
and hair is old like theirs. There's something not right
about them, they can't say what, like the pin
prick sensation they feel when, in winter, a cold
wind seeps through chinks in their walls. They feed
them boiled cabbage and bacon chunks, a stew

already cooking on their stove, and a wine that indeed
is most poor but much better when filled anew
each time they finish a glass. A miracle. They know,
at last, who the beggars are and ask if it's so,

have they dined with gods? The two nod and give
them one wish. They reply, To die together, never
either to have to mourn for the other or to grieve.
Waves crash against the headlands. Light, water,
ocean are holy to them, sunset, the cry
of sea birds as they fly overhead. They're unafraid
of dying, they agree, as the gods disappear, like a sigh
heard late at night that maybe one lover has made
and then rolled over to sleep more soundly. As quickly,
they become two rocks, apart but together, islands
in a becalmed Pacific, craggy, rough-hewn, the sea
lit by luminous clouds, by a light that stands
outside the world, as gods do who've turned them into
stone, black as magma, gradually, over centuries,
to erode, to wash away, yet two altars, two

rocks, two lovers arising out of misty water, souls,
not shades or shadows. Ask the sand they will
become how it is like the sea or a shell like a wave,
how the dead recall the life they had, the bell tolls
of their days, and they will answer, We are the still-
ness within rivers, tides, winds, a sea-carved cave,
a storm, breezes on a sunny day, rustling leaves.
A wolf, a fox cub thankful for the meat it gnaws,
a bird soaring in air, a meteor, a cat's claws
teasing twine, a child on a swing, lovers lying side
by side, a father with his child on his back, a bride
awaiting her groom, a mother her baby, the crucified
one burning with desire, Ulysses re-sailing the ocean–
all will reply the same. Love moves without motion,
like stones in deep sea currents, altars to compassion.

Winter Solstice

1.

All is white. A woman on a gurney. His own gown
(open in back), the curtains, walls, a clock face
and hands, the buzzing light above him. White. Down
a hall, nurses murmur.   A muffled laugh.   In a trace
of a sigh, he hears a northern breeze in late
winter.   Noon is bleaching the sky. His mind's
a blank, blurred as the spinning colors of a wheel,
the no colors of words. What is his name, his date
of birth? There's no him left to speak of. As he winds
through corridors, the floors he walks on tip like the keel
of a ship. Back in bed, he flips on his side, bites
on a bit with a hole for a tube. White waves. His sight's
set northward.   White tides roll in. He is trying to stay
in the Arctic. Snow is blissful. The white nights of Norway.

2.

The sun is hiding in a field of mice and corn stubble.
A chill wind. The old man wheezes in his bed.
He struggles up from his swaybacked mattress. Trouble
is coming. It is Satan down the road, his eyes red,
glowing above the horizon, below the pine stand.
Cold seeps through his windows, cripples the hand
the Lord has blessed. He has healed the infirm, ill,
and broken, not by his skill, but by God's. It is a miracle
he has stayed saved and sin-free. Oh, preacher man, who knows
righteous anger, the gospels by heart, the folly
of these times, the Word, who, in the dark, shows
the way: your grandson, scion of your blood–see
what you've done–his drawers torn down to his knees,
his cheeks lipstick smeared, lies unrisen like the sun in trees.

Vespers on Point Reyes

A Germanic sunset, Nachtstücke, black,
passionate, foreboding, seductive. Take
my hand. Here where we are stand-
ing is continent's end. Faraway, others wake
as we prepare for sleep. Come back.
Be a romantic with me. To evening. Abendland.

A last streak of light breaks through clouds
that darken the sky with their smoldering ash.
Faith is a man taking his last breath,
saying yes to it all as a nurse wash-
es his brow while outside twilight sounds,
in the lack of birds, its volkslied of death.

The sea is blacker than Wotan's patch, the sun
tiny, shining like a pin's head. Sublimity
is its fire, its ball of light, however small,
the glory of leaving. It is never easy
to vanish. The world's dying is never done
with nor its beauty, the romance of nightfall.

Play the last sonatas of Schubert, Brahms'
late intermezzos, Reger's clarinet
quintet. Listen after, in the silence,
in memory, every twilight, sunset,
how all whom you have loved are out of harms'
way. Whose arms hold you tighter in their absence.

To a Friend Who a Fundamentalist Christian Friend Said Was Doomed to Perdition

A plank walkway leads to the estuary
where an incoming tide rustles reeds
and cattails growing out of a bog.
There's no moon. The sky is cloudy.
Early morning breezes blow through trees.
Thick weeds crackle like a fire as they shake.
It's a monkish solitude here where Douglas fir,
redwoods, ever-flowing tidal waters
are disturbed only by the rare rumbling
of semis traveling on Sir Francis Drake
carrying full milk cans and crates,
braking at the curve by an isolated shack.
At dawn, sunrise burns the hills,
scrub trees, and summer dry grasses
while to the south a billowing fog spills
over them like a tide refilling the sea.
More than a century ago, a vast crack,
plates clashing, forced this lay of earth
northward like an island broken off
from the mainland. It was violence
that made this good place. Neither birth
nor death: to know nothing, to understand
nothing but what's heard in its silence.
A heron is fishing in shadows of the vanishing dark,
a stick figure in silhouette, tall and stark,
quietly stalking its prey. It moves
so slowly it seems without motion.
Birdsongs, a waylaid long billed curlew's,
a sparrow's warbling, a junco's trilling.
Breaking day's awakening those still dreaming.
The tide's retreating to the Pacific ocean.
And the white heron, with a fish in its beak,
flies over reeds to a sand spit near where
the bay ends by Route One to disappear
from spying eyes. What does it mean

to revere a bird? Dead fish, fed heron?
Or a slight, solitary snake camouflaged, the green
of the grass through which it slithers
toward shade, away from day's dangers,
sparkling like a diamond necklace
from the sunlight shining off its dew-slick scales?

Beachside Entries, #1

If all this is as it is intended to be, nothing else matters. Stern old men in nightshirts close shutters against bad weather. On the outer islands where pelicans and terns flock for refuge, the water rises slowly, but steadily. Men dressed like women clop down cobble stone streets in the quarter, turn corners, and, though it is barely past noon, disappear forever.

Panting dogs drink air. On the bus, Joe or Scott hunts for the address Phil left him of Don whose lover now lives alone and bereft in the rooms upstairs. Party animals play in the park games whose rules they are too drunk to remember. No one knows their names. No one knows the names of the children who live in caves by the river either, though their father is rumored to be alive and fabulously rich.

In the centre of town, cats are herded like rabbits into hutches and slaughtered for their meat and fur. Officials consult experts whom no one believes. They say the only certainty is that the water has not yet gone bad, but strange stains streak the skin of the handsomest faces.

No one knows when the next boat leaves. No one knows why there is so much talk. The movie is an old one, the sets from the South China Sea.

Beachside Entries, #8

What really moved me about Jim, Don says, was the way he always nodded his head politely when he smiled. We were all strangers together on that last leg of the journey here and acted like strangers, afraid and alone, no one speaking to anyone. But the stories of violence afterward that were widely reported were not true.

None of us knew who set that first explosion, though later we watched the things that had hurt us burn, cheered, and threw more fuel on the fire. The newspapers said that the city fathers had met all night with counsel in private session only to emerge from their chambers, like Jim's father from his den with those photos he had found in Jim's dresser to demand, "What is the meaning of this?"

And that was all. The old life was over. At first, because we were unused to freedom, the city bewildered us, yet gradually we grew accustomed to it, like an adolescent to his body. Jim liked the beaches best where love, like the fog, would burn off about noon.

He enjoyed his job, the gym, and a good party. After the second parade, we found the right apartment and moved in together without illusions about its lasting. Why should we have let paradise confuse us?

The trick of any religion is to formulate its doctrines so obscurely that they cannot be understood and then expect unwavering faith. Summer will come again anyway and each year's vacation. I remember the river best and the naked men who gathered there and Jim's dream of building a cottage right on the beach where the water bent back to the west.

Beachside Entries, #23

You have only begun to mourn. Come away, fellow sailors. In this part of the world, at this time of year, night falls early. A friend calls and, even before he begins to tell you, you already know what he has to say and leave the book unread for days. Come away.

They should never have gone out in this weather. Do you know one among them who was not unjustly punished, who you did not think had merely gone out ahead of us and would be coming home again? But they do not rest in their father's house. Come away.

Look westward, where the first light can be seen on the higher hills spilling onto the lower ones in the east. Waiting there for the school bus, the boy drenched by the rain despite his too large yellow slicker is you, ashamed of the sentimentality implicit in such a disguise, crying out inside, "Do not make me have to go through this again."

On board the ship, he sees his old companions, those boyhood friends cast off with him so long ago, their faces shadowed by the same shocked look of loss and incomprehension as haunts children captured by pirates.

In a popular story they told to one another to ease the long journey, a mother sits on a screened porch paring apples, squinting towards the sea secretly, like someone afraid of appearing too hopeful. But the message when it arrives is only more bad news and lies. Their life is hard. Their captors fight among themselves. There is no talk of ransom.

A Poem Beginning with a Man Floating on Water

1.
As stones or pebbles below the surface know desire, seeking
the freedom of air, a man longs to be water. His body floats
dreamily, sky and lake one, undivided, the slim horizon blurred,
smudged gray.

A half lit sphere floats too, a lunar dream perhaps as the light
and shadows of his reveries loom over the lake. His flesh
reflects the moon, its watery double as easy to see though.
Suspended in air, a hole cut out of it, rimmed by light, a carved
circular stone is dark as the man's black eyebrows and beard.

Say a man sleeping in a lake dreams of a ring, some perfectly
made thing unfound in nature, what only a mind and hands can
create. Say it is an image of itself that his body most needs,
that he often dreams of.

A rock transformed into a stony amulet hangs in the sky, a
talismanic guide to what living means, the circle of light and
dark, glove and ring, the order of things drowned in water like a
snake taken by the sea, an engulfed island or cathedral.

May a man's body be buoyed up by the deep, unsinking in
peace, undrowning in a lake as he dreams of a paradisal calm, of
a sea's timelessness?

2.
He comes in disguise, like emptiness, the void heard in unsaid
goodbyes. The day is fogged-in. I can barely see three feet
ahead unless I'm wrong and it is night when he enters my room.

He is a guy dressed in black jeans with a scruffy black beard or
a ghost, a phantom I can believe in if I am sleepy enough. His
face is postered on the wall. When I feel lost, I concentrate on
it or on his black jeans. On the floor, by the foot of my bed, I
hear weeping.

Then I see her head, her haunches, her right rear paw. I tickle behind her ear. She used to like that. There's a wind sifting through trees. It makes a crackling sound to remind me how she didn't like sand blowing in her eyes or the ground shifting under her feet while we walked on the dunes.

I hear my own crying as if it were someone else's, my father's. I remember his defying death, outlasting his diseases, a stone in a raging creek until it washed him away into the water he had been seeking to flow into since before he was born.

3.
All mourning aspires to constancy. Refusing to be comforted, it claims every life is like a Greek ship's stern, a plow that breaks the sea like earth. I've read that somewhere. Or watched it on clips from a movie.

Exiled at birth, refugees tell tall tales to pass the time. My mother's grief won't mean anything when there is no one left to recall it. Without brothers, I walk in nothing, in air, in clearest air.

"It's time," my mother said and died. The way of paradise is unrenewable and never lies. The meadow I live near demands I obey it, says, "Go home to where you were born."

I refuse to leave here. Despair is too enticing, a tail biting snake that must devour itself to survive. I wonder who is seducing whom. My mother said a dream is a creek that runs through a wide green field gathering tears until it becomes a stream, a river, and flows, all sorrow repealed, into the sea: mare, timelessness, agape.

4.
It is raining, good weather for disbelieving in reality. Dense thickets in woods, mist streaming from a waterfall. It is my last summer. Childhood is over. I reek of sod, oak roots, needles, brush. A pool. A cascading creek cut from rock.

I have lost my time for endless play. Rhododendron petals swirl in the froth. I left my bike at the trail head. Zigzag twists over the pass, then a long hike to where I can ride again, the long trip home, the unsafe roads and highway.

I remember this forty years later. Robert smells good, like pine. I beg him wait to wash it off his sweaty skin. It tastes like resin, his body as wild as faraway woods. Sometimes a loss is forgotten until it returns like a lover.

I am caught by the half-light in the pine forest around my lake. I want dreams to stay. To keep singing strangely. I want water to mean everything.

Thera

1.
On grotto walls, in frescos they've survived.
Boys boxing, hooked fish, a silver unicorn,
blue birds, monkeys, cinch-waisted, bare-breasted
women. Listen. Krimon calls to Amotion

who is racing to him. In a cave, after making
love, they cut their names like graffiti
in the rock face of a mountain, left nothing
but ruins when Thera exploded into the sea.

2.
Sunrise. He longs for Apollo, his light
to come, for love, its daybreak brilliance
to enter him. Cloudless skies, the insight
that comes from perfect days, the radiance

of the sea-, white-washed Cyclades. His holiday
is almost over, his summer's devotion.
Thera has taught him to worship, to pray
to the Mediterranean as if to Poseidon.

Women's hoop earrings, braided hair,
skirts embroidered like tapestries,
their graceful dancing, wine, bright fair
skin, almond eyes. Floral intricacies,

lithe ferns, dolphins flying over ships
oared to harbor. Sienna dark men,
handsome, bold shoulders, string-thin lips,
blue hair, black ringlets. He had lived well then.

Its grapes still sweeten his tongue. The sun
is white, the sea tarnished copper's blue-greens,
still water's silver mirror. The island is a profusion
of tesserae, fragments of ancient scenes,

the man he had been four millennia before
his birth, found, restored, images
exposed or extracted from rubble like ore
from a pit, carved names, chiseled messages.

3.
By Delphinios, Krimon had sex with a boy,
the brother of Bathykles. Timagoras and O.
and Empheres had sex here. Older than Troy,
names scratched into Mesa Vouno.

Kallisté. Most beautiful island. Sacred
to Zeus, the Charities, Persephone, Hermes,
a crescent moon seaborne, naked
as these lovers: Rheksanor, Arkhagetas, Prokles.

Penelope Weaving After

As she works, her loom sounds like the sea
lapping on beaches, pebbles pinging,
caves in the cliffs echoing breezes'
sighing, her maids gossiping by a door.

The waiting, the pitiful delay of her life,
daytime weaving, the counterpoint
of thread within thread, by night the music
of its unmaking, softer than sleeping.

The scene she repeats of his returning,
of Argos dying, of her embracing him,
mist enfolding them like a cloud a god
sends to save his favored from death.

Thgkk, thgkk goes the shuttle. She's weaving
out of yearning, out of need, as hungry
as a spider spinning its web, longing
to catch the past, to trap it in her tapestry,

to restore him by what she fabricates
to end her waiting, though he has left
to meet a fate more mortal than Troy's,
wandering where nothing woven in cloth

could entangle him as she'd hoped before.
Homeless, parched, sun-blistered, roaming
deserts for a place to plant his oar,
he's the madness of memory, the love inside her.

All suitors are sadly dead. And she,
unravelling at night what she weaves by day,
shuttle renewing the intricate fabric
she afterward ruins, who is she, if not made

and unmade by the passion she creates only
to undo it, how it returns by leaving,
the weft over and under the warp
threaded, unthreaded, and always the pain.

Hippolytos Rising out of the Sea

Had wild Hippolytos Leander seen,
Enamored of his beauty had he been.
That's Marlowe. Waves, beaches, love.
The Mediterranean's. The dream time
of its islands. Suppose Poseidon saw
in the sea's shimmering mirror above
its currents, not himself, but the sublime
sight of a boy. And he, who was the law
over waters, ordered his horses away
to save him, spilled his seed in the sea,
and put (Marlowe again) Helle's bracelet
on his arm, vowing never to harm
him. Tanned limbs, thighs, chest. To be
embraced by swirling riptides. Say,
too, the sun was enamored, early set
below the sea to hold him. Or Phaedra.
Artemis. Fire, icy earth. The alarm
he felt to be adored by the elements,
to be drowned in water as a testament
to the sea, as Poseidon's sexy sacrament.

Neptune was angry that he gave no ear,
And in his heart revenging malice bare.
I was twelve, Chris sixteen when he adopted
me, new next door neighbor, my bedroom
window across from his. High Rock, Crystal
Lake, swimming holes where we waded
or swam, outdoor pools, the half light gloom
of locker rooms, a cascade lined with tall
granite walls and honeysuckle, wildflowers,
brushwood. I haven't seen him for sixty
years. Yet, look, he is stepping out of a pool
or a lake or the sea, somehow still towers
over me, Chris, Hippolytos, famous for deny-
ing women, dark hair dripping, eyes onyx
flaked, having almost drowned, a fool

for diving straight down, his legs entangled
in bottom feeding weeds, a lake's dirty tricks,
but surviving, released, rising again
onto a beach. Do you remember us then,
Chris, both sea-saved? Lovers of water. Lovers of men.

Selinus' Son, #1

In Botticelli, wind blown Aphrodite steps ashore
out of Ouranos' shell. She cups her right hand
modestly over her right breast. Her left hand
and a swath of unshorn golden hair conceal her vulva.
Dressed in a gown dotted with cornflowers, a nymph
holds a daisy sown mantle to robe her nakedness.
But this is Lissos, Nineteen Ninety Six. The cloak
Selinus' son Nikos wears is a cloud
dissolving into mist, a white light from which
he is being born, an archaic wild beauty,
a naked bearded kouros, stepping onto a rock,
on ancient marble strewn ground. At night, he sleeps
under a sky said to have revealed to Plato, "Men die
because Time cannot love them as it loves itself."

Selinus' Son, #3

If we should peer beyond what is ours to see,
with deeds and mouth utter blasphemies,
never fear the gods, trespass sacred places,
profane the sea, sky, olive groves, grape vines,
pine, spirit of the fruit of ivy, wild selino,
if we defy justice, stain the good with folly,
fail the feast days, lay hands on untainted
things, how can we dance or holily grieve?
The gods are long gone, their temples ruins
for millennia. Yet still he turns his torso,
its tragic form. No ode to sing, no flute
to follow, he alone is left of the chorus. His hands
grip his head and hair, his muscles taut
with sensual despair, reverent of the rites.

Orphée et Eurydice

1. The Descent

Woods in morning light, trees' weighty limbs
struggling to stretch skyward, pine,
live oak, scrub brush, the sweetly acrid
odor of persimmon rotting on a forest floor.

A brown fox hunting for rabbits, squirrels
stuffed with nuts scrambling up hickory.
He pauses by a pond fed by a creek, kneels,
notes clouds floating, geese flying by in their V

while a gap like a crevasse opens along
a stream's swelling bank. He hikes down
its ledge, boulders for borders, its walls
dark and moist as a cave, somnolent and cold.

He must save Eurydice, death like a struck
bell tolling inside him, slowly reverberating
into silence, the temple within him,
monks chanting prayers wordless as birdsong.

In his fear, he hears the voices of specters
echoing in his soul, mournful as a creek in
an August dry spell lamenting summer,
end of year leaves resisting hibernal winds.

She stands motionless, eyes-closed, dark
as the dead of night, a Buddha carved
out of a coal-black cliff or painted
on a silk screen in the pain of her solitude.

Hades, he sees, is matter dissatisfied, the floor
of Death's kingdom littered with broken bones
petrified faces, calcified lives like a shoreline
after a storm strewn with driftwood and shells.

A river divides them, rust-stained and cold,
its banks poorly lit by dimming fires, flames
reduced to embers and ash, twilight's last rays,
the Orphée he glimpses in the mirror of her eyes.

2. The Return

Burning, burning, a ravishment
beyond returning,
a relinquishment, a bliss
like the bite of a snake.

Beneath a stone-chiseled sky,
like a wild child,
Orphée cries
for the soul he's lost,

the light that might
revive her,
Eurydice who knows
the way they must take,

he to follow,
trust in her guidance,
rebirth
beckoning upward,

she a smoldering darkness,
a winter morning,
clouds sighing as they clash,
a grief in the wind

until on earth
daybreak hovers,
mist dissipates
like ghosts at dawn,

spring lifting sky-blue hills
to a renewed sun,
rivers flowing
toward forgotten seas,

Eurydice, Orphée,
loss, song
reborn as one,
the hell of her dying on fire inside him.

Possession

Via Appia. Unlike Daphne, he pines to be free.
HIs skin is cypress bark; hair, leaves, moss scattered
by wind; fingers turned into tangled twigs. To be
a boy again. Wooed. God-flattered.
No bird's nests in his eyes. No tree-bound slavery.
His roots exposed on the earth are battered
by legionnaires' feet and weaponry. To see
himself as a god had adored him, clothes tattered
and torn by passion. Now he is greenery,
the seasons, cones' seeds. What mattered
to him was to survive like his pursuer, immortality,
yes, but to be always young, like the god who ardently
possessed him, fucked him once, splattered
his loins, his trunk dew-wet, sap-spattered:
so you, a boy, a tree in a wayside wood
in perpetual spring, flowering in dreams as you should,
and I, no god, long past the frenzy we once knew,
retrieving a myth of desire, needing it to find you.

Shard

Three Greek letters, Rho, Eta, Psi,
engraved into a marble shard the size
of a man's palm, found in the Syrian
desert by a 'Nam vet on his long way
home from the war, worn smooth by sand
and wind and time, chipped and gray.

I met him in 'Sixty-eight at Dean's.
I can't recall his name, only the jeans
he wore, the tight t-shirt, his hair
disheveled, hippie long, and dark,
his eyes pale gray like the shard, his fair
skin, the scar formed like a question mark

on the right cheek of his face, a sign,
a rune he might have drawn to define
who he was, like a tattoo, lividly
inked, a wound that grew redder when
he smiled, more unreadable, no key
to anything, like the letters men

had incised in stone to spell words, now
a shattered whole that won't allow
decipherment.

                I've lost it. He gave it
to me, tossed it into my lap, said,
"Keep it." I did for forty years. Then it hit
me today. It's vanished as if it had fled

from me, undeserving of his gift, the body
he meant by his gesture to offer me,
too, and I afraid of the meanings he hid
on it, inside it, I wasn't sure which,
like those letters that exposed no word
on the rock he'd found, dug up from a ditch,

and pocketed. This is not a myth,
this story, or the secret of a hieroglyph
well kept. It is about the stone the heart
I've lost is, the fragment of something
ancient I've wasted, passion, the smart
of the chisel on the marble of it, cutting, carving.

Res publica

The falling moon looks wrapped in gauze,
a forty watt bulb dimmed by cotton cloth,
the soft light color of balsa wood.
A man is a slight thing if he lacks a cause
to make his city more righteous.   Both
land and sea are gray this morning, good
for watching the moon decline, turning white
as the snow on which it glows in an unplowed
field, pale as a helmsman's face
blanching at new storms to follow. Nothing is right.
Civility is drowned off the beaches. Loud
as troops marching at a steady pace,
the waves know no retreat, no low tides.
The moonlight fails before it can reach
the water, hides behind a wall of chalk white
clouds, then slips from the sky. Every side's
truth's foe, what history should teach
a schoolboy. Cicero waits in plain sight,
his face, bald pate pallid from being old,
not frightened. A man should speak freely
if a citizen of Rome. Yet how grimly night
holds him. And Seneca, as he has been told
he must, tests the bath water to see
if it is hot, his knife faintly golden by moonlight.

The City Their Blood Had Built

Irredentism, the bough the tree gives him,
the path down the earth shows him,
the pages his book opens to,
the photos in it,
the grove that lights his way
as if its leaves could shine like torches
by the cave's mouth,
the haunting sound
of long missed voices whispering,
the spirit that glows
from ghosts like twilight in woods,
their tears, what grieves under ground,
in an echoing grotto,
some other Troy, the past he has lost,
forests depopulated, chopped, toppled,
his last glimpse of it still burning, crackling
in his head, its towers on fire,
courthouse, school, steeple,
his world over the sea,
the plain where he had battled to stay
now in ruins like the shades he hears,
sighing to him as if from wind-carved craters:
  Fate is a disaster,
  for even you who live
  must move as restlessly as water,
  flicker like us
  in subterranean caverns, unfree,
  each of our names by steady rains eroded
  from every gravesite,–
  you who can't know in the days to follow
  what might befall you
  save missing the friends death has taken,
  no Aeneas, no hero, unsure of the future,
  no Rome to found, who seek after them,
  wanting them home,
  in memory, in the house

where you live by the sea,
listening to the waves that tell
the silenced history
of the dead, those who stay or roam
alike doomed by an unfulfillable prophecy,
the foretold re-birth
of everything you had believed had worth
in your storied, fallen, irredeemable city.

May 30, 1593

1.

All day I have watched my king die
in bright lover's pain. In my house,
in a room with ox-thick walls
I listen to the songs of prisoners

as I wait for a queen to strip me.
The air is close. There is no fire.
I have been dreaming of hounds
near a moonlit pool and the shy gaze

of a boy and the black wood
where I hid as a child in the mild
years after the wars. In the days
before the plague, I made kings

lie in state on stage and cracked
gold heads for food. My enemies
burned. As their fires sought
speech, I turned their words to blood.

When with a pen I impaled
King Edward in the castle's sink,
I clutched pillows and sweat out
the night. I have kissed the heads of traitors

and slept with wolves, but the breath
of man and beast is always cold.
Children haunt me, my poems' scars,
the words left on flesh of my soldiers

suffering. The stench of human breath
chokes my voice as I cry for a lover
to build a castle on my bed and crown
my sex with flowers. Instead, I sail

with Drake for pearls. Edward, all day
I have watched the tough peers chop
your lover Gaveston on Blacklow Hill
and begged them stop this treason

to their Lord, my king. Killed in a tavern,
stabbed in my eye with my knife,
I condemn with my last breath
my assassins to the Tower's terror,

pain long and hard or screw or rack,
any device an artist might choose
to use, subtle or crude, that in his hands
would prove more magical than life.

2.
Ta rum, goes the drum despair.
A goose swallows a hog, a snail
rides a dog, the cock steals a fox,
in a stream fishes are boiling.

A sip of blood, a kiss. When it shines
sere, the sun is red as lips,
chop-cherry ripe and sweet as figs.
In fields, Fergus Falsetongue's fair

fresh oxen plough until the sky
turns pear yellow, damson, grape
pulp, posset, and Hecate's
russet-eyed horses Stadlin

and Hellwain, errant past the moon,
gallop in a glass. Though flesh
is folly, music is a spirit and a heavenly
body is found in night's every sound.

Sleep now, my Kit, though rest calms
no fright. God, swaddled in clouds

like a Titan's monstrous child,
rocks you in his welcoming arms.

For the Chymical Marriage of John Dee and Edward Kelley

Astraea is my Queen, Welsh like her wizard.
Groenland, Estetiland, the land of the Frisians
and all of Arthur's twenty kingdoms I would give
her and call my Britain Brutanicae, the latter Troy

and go with Orpheus and Plato to Egypt,
star-demon in search of my star, or sit
quiet with Lull on Mount Randa and wait
for the dignity of the Lord. With numbers,

I teach his mysteries and chant their measures
in verse. I hope to see God and have built
the greatest library in England. Fearful
navigators seek me, Mercator's friend,

to plot their safest course for the America
I call Atlantis. I set my sights further
and east. In a single bitter storm, I lost
claim to most of Canada. Once in Glastonbury,

seeing the past summoned into a single tomb,
I thought my body sang from the sins of the flesh,
the great stain that would soon destroy me
when sun and moon conjoined with Aries

ascendent in prodigious light. I hope to see
God. But all my life has been visionless save
when I had for scryer coarse Edward Kelley,
ignorant and a liar, wily as angels in their deceit.

Henry James in the Bois de Boulogne

The subtleties he finds in spring's breezes,
the Bois' waters' piping voices,
bustling leaves. A dowager's satin
shawl, her silk skirts. A rose that pleases
with its restraint.   A child who tosses
his cap tree high as he plays with a thin
stick and artful hoop. A boy reading
a book while leaning on a cedar. Nothing.
Nothing wild. A park's a rare artifice,
a refinement of a nature he'd prefer
stay hidden, the rapture, the madness of passion.
In impressionist grays, Parisian clouds erase
the sun. He fears the threat of bad weather,
more war talk. Who paces the Bois like a prison.

History as a Hobbyhorse

See the child nestled in his bed
against the gunfire in his head.
You, your daddy is dead.
Hop-hop, the hobbyhorse.

His ash blond silk-thin baby
hair flutters in the wind. No Mutti
comes. None will, blood-drowned.
Hop-hop, the hobby horse.

The moon drips in the village well
forgetfulness like a magic spell
that makes of hell a heaven again.
Hop-hop, the hobby horse.

Each night the world is orphaned by
a gun that kills without remorse.
Yet in the dark a child still rides,
hop-hop, his wild hobbyhorse.

Throwing a Wreath into Pearl Harbor

Pearl is burning. As Saipan's plains burn, civilians
hiding in caves, shooting, strangling their children,
leaping from cliffs, innocents, the thousands
dying in mass suicides; burns on the day when
General Saito proclaims to his men, In death there is life,
and, with his ceremonial sword, commits seppuku
as an adjutant shoots him; burns, by bullet and knife,
when an officer kills his men, beheading them who
began to die when their Zeros hit Pearl. It is the way
of wars never to end. No soldier can surrender.
The men struck at dawn at Pearl or under the midday
glare on the Bataan road are there for the slaughter
over and over. All violence is prophesy.
Pearl burns. So Okinawa burns. Now as then. Nagasaki.

Christmas, 1972

Suppose it were possible that myths could be real,
our fictions as true as you and I are, as readers
are when they believe in a story, in their hearts feel
the lives writers make up, all inveterate dreamers,
that it happened–the virgin birth in a barn or a cave,
angels singing of a child to shepherds, wise men
wending their way from the distant east, brav-
ing dangers, bringing gifts, kneeling sheep and oxen–
that a fable could replace the violent Christmas day
when I was thirty and lived in the country far
from town and had quit the party inside to explore
the earth for auguries of peace, what birds might say
by traces left in snow as the wind blew and they soar-
ed out of sight and bombs fell on 'Nam to end the war.

Santiago

1.

Santiago is our city, built on ruins, rubble,
the dead, unexcavated grave sites
below high rises, apartments that resemble
Manhattan's or London's. Urban lights

have replaced stars and moon. The bridge across
the river you wanted to walk on with me
is my refusal, fearful your life is my loss.
I am black, you are a changeable gray.

Our passions' two colors foretell the day
you will go. I sense under my feet
the men before me, the casual way
they had quit you in a dive on an unlit street.

2.

Smell the grit, the dirt on men's hands,
the sweat on faces, in armpits. Pity's
how a road should be mapped, by garbage cans,
refuse bins, the sewers under cities.

It is not foolish for the body to be led
by desire. The old places are visible
still, rocks from a subway that astonished
you, almost Incan, easily chipped, friable.

Like mortal men, an expiring world takes
its time to die. Find me again.
The season is quickly thinning, lakes
we swam in gone dry from lack of rain.

3.

You loved women. I never could or did,
not in your way. I would wait for sunset

to head to the bar where I found you hid-
den in a back room one night, anxious, who let

me kiss you as I had dreamed of while a stream
of men passed us, me sinking in them,
in you, who pushed me away, seem-
ingly straight, the music playing my hymn

to you, steady beat, thumping rhythm
of a synthesizer like waves pounding
bridge pilings, cocks risen, jism
later spewed in water: me diving to you swimming.

4.
The legends are not wrong, men like you surviving
by escaping across the bridge, though
it is a rougher life they are now living,
stains on their clothes, tears they sew and re-sew,

rips, the fraying that tough work has caused.
You are walking on El Puente de Despedidas.
Will you return to me? I thought you had paused,
looked back, exchanged gray for black. No más.

I am studying the neighborhood's oldest maps,
tracing your journey, why you have had to leave,
my embraces a dare, my kisses traps
to keep you, a last "No" my sole way to grieve.

5.
All passion is a chant before sunrise, what is
real, unstoppable, that sanctifies the world,
makes it holier, a man abandoned, his
hopes denied him, mine by women that hurled

you from me. I followed your route. I watched
you walking not to get away, but to be
less ruined, to return some day, touched
by my hands, my lips, your wanting to see

more clearly the rooms we might dwell in, poorer
but more free, seeking to renew what waits below
you, what you had seen in water flowing under
the bridge, enough rubble there to restore Santiago.

After Holding the Man

Because of old snapshots, a book, a movie,
I grieve for two boys, men I never knew.
I should tell you of my friends whose lives
were cut short. Who are who I am in ways
I don't understand, their pasts what I see
most clearly. Death is never through
with you, the bodies, the faces, what survives
in loss, the sorrows of all days.

I should tell you how they live
near me, by the beach, the sea
where my home is, playing, swimming,
making love. How much they give
back freely, beckoning me
to join them in the feast they bring.

This. This wet, gray stone
I grasp in my hand, chipped,
pocked, weather-worn that I
tripped on is my heart, my
ancient, cold lone-
liness, torn, ripped
out of me, this useless, cast-off thing,
dull rock, the enormity of all I'm missing.

The Amalfi coast. Sorrento.
Blue sky, no clouds, azure sea.
Smooth white pebbles at low tide,
wave-washed rocks. Me below.
High above on a cliff, you, who have died.
The stone I throw you the love denied me.

Mitsein

Curious, isn't it, how easy it is to say, "The ground
of Being," and not know what it means. Two photos
of you I've kept help me remember. Time leaves
behind as it moves ever onward the haunting sound
of voices missed whispering with a music that glows
like Callas you said, like clouds at night. What grieves
me most about our long lost talks are the earth, people
you loved who are ghosts now, too, forests chopped, toppled,
depopulated. There's a burning, crackling in my head
like buildings on fire, courthouse, school, steeple.
You, my philosopher friend, my preacher, teacher
of absurdities. Volatile. A staunch believer
in God, you'd insist, and laugh at me, at yourself,
for what we knew ought not be true, you and your bookshelf
of ironies. Talk as philosophy, words an onrushing river.
I yearn for a world over the sea, a peerless, unafraid
city, paradisal, peaceful. You're a shade who has made
plain to me often since you died, "Death is no disaster,"
by which I suppose you mean you flow like water
or roam in woods as if time were a wilderness free
as a mountain you climb to build on its summit
a house made of stone, no monument, just a space
to dwell in before you depart for some other place
stranger than the one we're born in. Where could it
be, save in the missing, missing, missing of life? Ground of Be-
ing? You are mine on this last day of the year. I don't mind
admitting I'm growing more confused by calendars. Some find
them imposing and hang them on a door, the important
moments ahead circled as I circle yours–the date
I always mark first, the one on which you left, disappeared
for good–whenever I pin a new one to a wall. I've feared
the night too long, my wandering friend, my half-mad Marco.
Rome,
I agreed, should prove a fine place to die in. That is, if by
'home'
you'd intended to cite a classical beginning. I live by the sea,

ancient Greek, in a way, like the shores of unknowing you
showed me.
My confusion is all I can offer to thank you. This plea disguised
as a poem.

In Praise of a Minor Poetry

Snow is what his poems mean, the surprising kind
coming in early spring, gentler than winter's,
the earth still warm from yesterday's sun,
thawing so fast no harm is done to flowers.
Behind his home, high over a spruce forest,
rises a craggy ice-capped mountain peak
the sun ignites each dawn like a match, struck
on rock, that the wind blows quickly out.
Such cold is what his poems want to say,
the strange chill of age from the day he was born,
the nip of fall in all he has loved, the words
of his lyrics chiseled from ice. That crystalline.
That light, impossible to touch or hold, like sleet
to a boy's delight melting in his hands.

Another Life

It's always dawn when I hear Jay's fear
during his last call to me, painful
every time, his whispering, coughing
still clear almost forty years later.

This morning, two surfers rescued a boy
from drowning. I walk the beach staring
as others ride their boards to shore
and quickly paddle back out again.

It's not that paradise is always a lie.
Or a fantasy. Like Tiberius's island,
Capri was the name of a bar where I'd go
when I came out late in search of pleasure.

The Stud. The Lion. The Rendezvous.
The seedy, sweat-drenched Rawhide.
Most of the men I knew then have died.
Every day I think of them. And Jay.

My ways have become ordinary. I live
in a beachside neighborhood in a house
that rests on sand near where Playland
once stood. Or I live in old memories.

I watched a film last night. A woman
was hanged unjustly in such terror
she needed to be doped and carried
to the scaffold. She'd had romantic dreams.

That she'd be happier than she was,
that the aurora borealis might shine nightly
in every sky, spring would never die,
and she'd live another life like this, but better.

Something Understood

When I was a boy, funerals were no place
for children. I was left at home to play
with friends. First grandmother Karen
died, then Louise. Gone, leaving no trace,
as if one day they had vanished. I'd pray
they would come to me. My hopes turned barren.
I stand on a hill of Bay View Cemetery
in Jersey City, a park, docks, the Hudson
below me. It is not what we ask of the dead
but what they ask of us that makes
us who we are. The river enters the sea,
emptying into it, as if its life were done
as ours must be at the end, having said
what it can. Cargo ships, one cruise liner
plow into the North Atlantic. To suffer
departure. What an ocean gives, it takes
back. I am watching its constant flowing,
feeling the tides, the currents, the unknowing
of dying inside me, its emptiness, as if bidden
to it. Not mine but the prayers I hear. "My son, my son."

A Drowned Man

I watched a man dying this dawn
or maybe he was already dead.
The rescue squad kept trying to save him
with CPR for more than twenty minutes.

Or far longer. I don't know.   Cop cars,
ambulances, a fire truck
were parked near the sea wall
when I and my dog walked past.

Pick-ups, vans, a bus whizzed by,
north and south.   Runners on
the median. A bike or two.
Some took time to look. Most didn't.

Two old homeless men were piling driftwood
for a fire near where I stood and stared.
No one attempted to stop or arrest them.
I left the spot because of the smoke.

Nature in its immensity. The stupefying earth.
From headland to headland, an encircling
vastness, imponderable, like someone
who'd ask of you no more than a kindness.

I spied upon a man in his dying. What am I,
in the aftermath? Ocean and sand
and sandy loam. The sea at its cruelest. Men
at their pain. This desecration, this useless poem.

The First Day of The Outside Lands Concerts

The beach's cold and misty as a Maine
coast's winter. Dozens of geese and pelicans
stand on their shadows, the sand rain-
glazed at low tide. Nothing happens.

What are they waiting for from the water?
Five young people rise out of dunes,
blankets draped like capes over
their shoulders, wrapped round like cocoons.

The concerts begin tonight in the park.
They're bedraggled, hopeful, poor,
must crash through fences after dark
when the wind blows hard as off a moor,

ruffling the feathers on ravens' backs,
necks, revealing their scrawny bodies.
The kids pick up their paper sacks,
stretch their arms, wipe sleep from their eyes.

Loose sand blows off the shore and over
the highway, coating tongues, stinging
skin. They hesitate, frown as if fear-
ful they'll not be able to hear the singing,

the bands, the groups they've hitched so far
to follow. A blinding fog has fallen
on the Sunset. The N Judah streetcar
clangs its bell, moving slowly. An omen.

Thousand thousands here for the superstars,
the gods of rock in the park. No surety
in this weather, like what gets said about wars.
No truth in the fog of it, only more folly.

A red-tailed hawk perches on a lamp post,
head cocked to heed, eager for meat.
That's all they need believe, at most.
Their ears must hear, their mouths must eat.

But what if they can't get in, fail
to penetrate the gates? See no bands?
Shiver instead in their blankets in gale-
sharp winds, for warmth holding hands?

A wasted trip, the long journey lost?
Or would they huddle in the cleft of a dune
listening like children, star-crossed
children, to music as if played on the moon

in the faraway park surrounded by chain-
link fences, kept out with no money
for tickets? Or through the mist, thick as rain,
to the music in fog? In the cold of each day?

Say what is faint, hazy is the only clarity.
What is dimly seen, not easily heard.
How I need to tell you what you mean to me.
How I long to name it but cannot find the word.

Improvisations on Poems by Han Shan

1.
A black pearl sky. Dark clouds, drifting.
A waning moon like lanterns in rain.

Dawn, when it comes, like autumn's
last light, a wind sharp as winter's.

At noon, I resume my exile, weak
as a newborn's my arms my only oarsman.

The water winds upriver between rock face cliffs
like a snake slithering through dew-wet grass.

You wait for me where mountain peaks are
white as your hair. Why dress in fine raiments?

Your letters sound a thousand sighs. Days end
where cranes begin their longest journey.

The past is a leaf fast drifting toward a waterfall,
a dog tied to a stake, a servant's well-kept lies.

2.
No more springtime bird-calls.
No more thoughts of my brothers.

No more gardenias blooming,
the perfume my mother wore for parties.

The Yadkin no longer flows steady and green
with the clarity of a thousand new streams.

Dawn-tinged pink clouds float in the sky,
lost as the songs of a hundred years.

3.
I look far off at Tamalpais' summit.
Pacific's tides wash smoke ash from shoreline.

To debate like philosophers with hills charred by fire.
To argue with wilderness how all is not right.

If only I knew why life reads like bad fiction.
If only I knew why I pursued the wrong way.

4.
I tell myself stories of lakes and streams,
how dreams resemble the mist in clouds.

Fall's first rain blows sand off the dunes
like dust from the world. It drenches my clothes.

So many decades since we all parted, friends,
lovers. I work at my desk like a wife at her loom.

5.
I think a lot about my early youth
when I read books in unhoed fields.

Before I knew it, those days ended.
I click on the light over my bed.

I've broken my ties with red clay,
with people who talked and knew nothing.

6.
Last night, in a story I made up to help me sleep,
I returned home to see my best friend.

I called. He turned his head to look with the eyes
of a man who had never known me. Dead

eyes. Wasp's waists. Stork's knees.
The rhythms of poetry still possess things.

Flowers scatter. Birds fly off. Tears
fall. And Paul no longer beside me.

7.
To live is a fantasy, a tale of Cold Mountain.
I lie alone behind dunes, their fissures folded like cliffs.

It is dark this side of the ocean.
Why is the mind near life's end not freer of clamor?

For years I have dreamed of a stone bridge,
a wet, twisting path, a rust-colored pond.

Of a city whose buildings were the colors
of crags in old hills. What years remain?

Some valleys are more beautiful the deeper
you enter. I grow older and do what I please.

The trees on Cold Mountain grow darker the brighter
the sun. The things we can't say, unstained.

Why do people want to be better? I am the letter
I never could write you, the story I left you untold.

Ringed Scales of a Snake

1.
Note how dark it is northward: the headlands,
Tam's summit, more obscure than night, drifting

like gathering clouds weighed down by sky,
shifting like boulders more massive than mountains

invisible until, like ink on black paper,
darkness spills upon darkness, soaking in.

2.
The Pacific is thundering, its waves breaking
loud as a cascade in the heights of the Sierra

where, trailside, watching rhododendron
petals swirl in a whirlpool of bubbles and foam

he dreamed of flowing like a flower downstream
to drown in the ocean three hundred miles away.

3.
Barely visible, white water churns as far
out as the horizon. No rain. More drought.

A man walking behind him clicks on
his flashlight. Three times his height,

his shadow falls where darkness
leaves nothing to hide in.

4.
Scattered lights on the sea, by shoreline
and cliffs. Improvisatory, transient,

a container ship's lit portholes,
crabbers' lanterns hung from masts

glow dim as candlelight. A flickering
to form a constellation from. To give a name to.

5.
Say: Moth dust. Waxwing's feathers. Ringed scales
of a snake. Kingbird's beak. Crockery shards.

Door bolt. Bear tooth. Mermaid's seaweed
hair. Twirling seeds. Grape pips. Flowering plum.

Night blinded things, lined up like stars. Each a sign.
Phosphorescent rocks. Pine stand. A dam's open sluice.

6.
Not where he walks, but how, sand sinking
beneath his feet, tide erasing his footprints,

dawn never to shine again, morning
arriving as night: sky, earth, sea

not freed into day but chained
like a lake in Siberian winter.

7.
No moon. No emptiness in its stead. No visible
pit in the sky. Solace comes in breeze's

kindness, the play of water in tide pools,
their starless gleaming slick as black silk,

incandescent, the blackened azure sky.
A crevasse between dunes, a streetlight blinking.

8.
To dwell in enlightenment and suspect day.
To know woods, hills, a river, eyes lit

by the visible, what illuminates them. Or to walk
on a morning darker than midnight,

the distance between them the words
he uses to plot their historical traces.

9.
To envision night flightless as a gimp bird.
Ink-dark water, barren hills, mountains

barred like a wrought iron gate. To see
shadows scattering. Waves crashing, swash

flowing, the coast jagged, sword-tip sharp.
To hear cliffs slowly shattering. Beseeching all.

10.
Night like a mountain twice climbed,
a river crossed, its dangerous portage.

Night like a way to a place elsewhere lost,
an unmanned boat drifting at sea.

Night like the wildness inside you, tendril
and vines thriving by clinging to rock face.

The Way Open to Other Ways

1.
The wind calms at first light. It is a seasonable
cold this morning. The tide is out, a lull
beachside after yesterday's storm. Dawn is a tale
of hills where the sun is delayed, of a full

moon that appears to be suspended
mythically in the sky, a radiance to it
as it lolls above the sea as if illuminated
by more than the sun, like a globe lit

from within. It is easy for a body to move
through the world when the air is so still,
so raptly quiet. Is there a light above
the sun's that some days decides to fill

the earth with splendor? Wood scents pass
freely through it, eucalyptus' wet bark,
Douglas fir's, redwood's, the grass,
sea oats, the fern trees in the park,

their resiny, pungent smells keener by day.
No crows are cawing, no songbirds singing.
What I'm seeing is like theater, a silent play
I have stepped into, a moon that is never setting.

2.
One pale dawn follows another, the steady
rains winter-heavy, the gutters on each street
clogged with brown leaves. Then, abruptly,
skies clear. Forsythia, jasmine compete

with gardenia, magnolia, camellias, azaleas,
jonquils, dogwood, red and snow white roses,
all blooming freely, their iridescent petals
flouting drab rules or whatever imposes

its cold order on nature. A garden, long
left to tend itself, is reviving. Spring birds
fly back, their songs mingling in one song
orioles, thrushes, chickadees. Tiny herds,

like cartoons, of squirrels, chipmunks scurry about
the yards, chattering, playing on trees,
showing what it means to be devout,
to see through your eyes what May sees.

3.
So far north, June shocks as in a Russian
novel. First winter thaws in shadows. Raw
mud turns new grass emerald.   Then the land
flares into the Chinese colors I saw

as the sun shone through crane-white clouds
on an ancient silkscreen, a monk, plain,
hog-fat, sucking plums, making no sounds,
quieter than lotus on the mountain. Plums stain

his robe wine-red. A boat waits by his hut.
In farewell, he embraces the farmer who hoes
his beds, its flowers topaz, agate.
If beauty is found in decay, winter snows,

in labor, the raked-over loam, the ice-
laden gates, then summer is paradisal. Past stone
walls and cliffs, his skiff flows. Rice
fills his bowl. It is twilight. Peace comes to everyone.

Sources

from Beachside Entries/Specific Ghosts:
Entries #1, #8, #23

from The Outerlands:
A Walk Down Mount Tamalpais, McAdoo Farm, Reunion, Randall
Jarrell, Herkimer Dolomite, Battenkill, In Praise of a Minor Poetry

from To the Final Cinder:
White Water Wind, #10, A Song of the Earth, Last Things,
Throwing a Wreath into Pearl Harbor

from Stone Altars:
Winter Solstice, To My Mother in Her Dotage and the Kindness
of the Lord, Michael's Gift, Stone Altars

from Late Summer Storm in Early Winter:
May 30, 1593, For the Chymical Marriage of John Dee and
Edward Kelley, History as a Hobbyhorse, Shard, Selinus'
Son #1, Selinus' Son #3, Hippolytos Rising from the Sea,
Christmas,1972, A Last Letter to John Baird

from Water's Eye:
A Poem Beginning with a Man Floating in Water

from The Return of What's Been Lost:
First Love: August 1959, Laguna Beach

from The Light of the Sun Become Sea:
Vespers on Point Reyes, Santiago, Thera, Possession, After
Holding the Man, Res publica, The City Their Blood Had Built,
Henry James in the Bois de Boulogne, The Way Open to Other
Ways

from Unbecoming Time:
Another Life, Something Understood, Woodlands, a True Story, The First Day of the Outside Lands Concerts, To a Friend Who a Fundamentalist Christian Friend Had Said Was Doomed to Perdition

from You Wait For Me Where Mountain Peaks Are White As Your Hair:
Penelope Weaving After, Ringed Scales of a Snake, Improvisations on Poems by Han Shan, Mitsein, A Drowned Man, Orphée et Eurydice

from Old-Growth:
Poem Set to a Line and End Words by Wordsworth, Redwood

Peter Weltner grew up in northern New Jersey and piedmont North Carolina. Throughout his youth, Manhattan was his holy city. He received an A.B. from Hamilton College and a Ph.D. from Indiana University and taught English Renaissance and British, Irish, and American Modern and Contemporary Literatures at San Francisco State University for 37 years. He lives with his husband, Atticus Carr, in San Francisco near the Pacific.